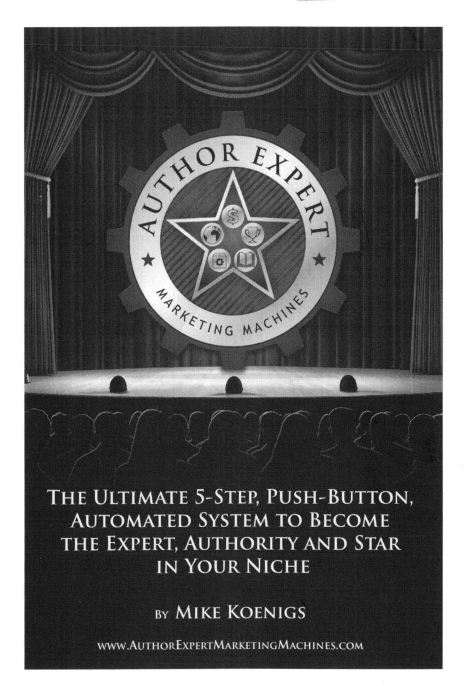

THE ULTIMATE 5-STEP, PUSH-BUTTON, AUTOMATED SYSTEM TO BECOME THE EXPERT, AUTHORITY AND STAR IN YOUR NICHE

BY MIKE KOENIGS

WWW.AUTHOREXPERTMARKETINGMACHINES.COM

This page intentionally left blank.

Author Expert Marketing Machines:

The Ultimate 5-Step, Push-Button, Automated System to Become the Expert, Authority and Star in Your Niche

Mike Koenigs

www.AuthorExpertMarketingMachines.com

VERSION 2.0

Table of Contents

Preface

Welcome. My name is Mike Koenigs and I want to take you on a journey to witness what I believe is the biggest opportunity since the Internet was invented.

That's a big fat, bold claim, and I WANT you to be skeptical. Having said that, I can promise that when you spend a few minutes with this book and the companion videos, you'll agree with me or at least experience a profound discovery about yourself.

If you don't know who I am or have never heard of me before, there's a short chapter and video you can watch to "meet" me and find out how I can help you become 2-5 times more valuable than you are right now and get paid what you're worth and what you deserve.

Here's that short video: http://0s4.com/r/MIKEK (that's a zero right before the "s", BTW)

Or scan this handy QR code:

I've spent nearly 25 years marketing top NY Times Bestselling Authors, celebrities and brands—and in this book, I'm about to give you the #1 secret—something that really is the "silver bullet" and "magic button" that can dramatically change your life and multiply your value when you apply some very basic principles.

Think about it like this: if I could give you a time machine where you could go back 10 years and keep all the knowledge and wisdom you have today, how would that change your life right now? Besides buying Apple Stock at $20 a share and Google stock, becoming filthy rich when you sold it, what if you could go back with the knowledge and know-how that would build your platform and make you a bestselling author or expert in any niche?

If you sold the Apple and Google stock, you'd probably spend all the money. It would most likely be gone, just like nearly every person who wins the lottery and finds themselves right back where they started a few years earlier. Most are in worse positions because they didn't pay their taxes.

But with the content in this book and the videos, you can be earning millions of dollars a year for the rest of your life. You could lose everything and with this knowledge, be right back in the game in a few months.

If you've been seeking and searching for years for the ANSWER, the SECRET that can literally turn around your personal and professional career, you've found it.

I discovered it recently when I faced the prospect of my own death when I was diagnosed with cancer. And when I decided to share this hard-earned knowledge and wisdom, it gave me the joy and freedom I was looking for too.

I want you to know you're not alone.

I'm here right now with you, because of you.
You're my passion and my purpose.

And if I had 30 days left to live, I'd be here with you right now.

Enjoy this book and the videos.

I'll see you on the other side of the screen.

Mike Koenigs

Author Expert Marketing Machines:

The Ultimate 5-Step, Push-Button, Automated System to Become the Expert, Authority and Star in Your Niche

Have you ever imagined yourself receiving an award on stage? Have you ever dreamed of delivering your message, product, idea or service to thousands or millions of people with incredible authority and credibility? What if you could be not only recognized for your talents, accomplishments, and expertise, but you could double, triple, or quintuple your income at the same time? Finally getting paid what you're worth and what you deserve…

If this describes you, I know what you're craving, what you're about, and where you'd like to go. What's more? I also know what's standing in your way.

My guess is you have a burning desire to contribute, to make a difference, to have massive impact and to help people. You're an entrepreneur, small business owner, author, expert, speaker, consultant, coach or creative type. And, most likely, you've been selling your time as a professional for 5, 10, 20, or maybe even 30 years. Maybe it's been enjoyable, maybe it's profitable, and maybe it's even rewarding, but at the end of the day, you are still punching the clock. When all is said and done, you are still *trading time for money...*

You know that there is more to life. You realize that your time is finite, that your income will forever be capped, and that there will be no way to expand your reach if you simply stay in the cycle you're in. You sense that there is an alternative, a better way.

You want to get paid more for your knowledge, know-how, experience, and expertise. You want to trade *real value* instead of time, to open up multiple revenue streams, and to proactively leverage all of the cash potential available in today's marketplace. You want and need LEVERAGE, freedom, control, and financial independence!

This book is about you becoming the expert, authority, and star in your niche whereby you communicate your message to the world and finally get paid what you're truly worth. Whether you've already published several titles, or you're just beginning, this may seem daunting. Fortunately, we've systematized the journey for you, by breaking it down into a five-step blueprint that will save you years of time, money, and effort.

The following pages are designed to turn your know-how and knowledge into a real business that gives you incredible influence, access, and authority—and makes you money

while you sleep...

 *The Opportunity*

I'm going to go out on a limb now. I have a feeling I also know *exactly why* you're struggling to succeed. I know why you have not yet been, "seen," "found," or "discovered." I know why your intent and efforts have not yet paralleled your efforts.

First and most importantly, know this—the problem is not *you*, and it's not *your message*.

Both the diagnosis and the cure for your business, professional, and personal challenge can be summarized in one simple word.

Are you ready?

The word is... *platform*.

That's it, platform. My hunch is—what you are currently lacking is a viable platform. No matter how great your message, story, or gift may be, no matter how great of an expert you are in your field, and no how much heart you have invested in your mission, it doesn't matter... until a large enough mass of people know you exist. You need a following, a vested group of people who care about you and what you have to say.

In this book, I'm going to do my very best to inspire you and give you the tools you need to get seen, found, and heard in ways you may have never dreamed possible.

I also want to give you a huge gift—I want to make you famous. I want you to be able to promote and market your products and services to the entire connected planet. As a start, I'd like to promote you to my list of nearly 250,000 prospects and customers, to promote you in our online store, to feature you in our $250,000 studio, and to give you an opportunity to speak at our next live event.

Are you intrigued?

I know that's a big, fat promise, and I know I'm going to have to prove my worth. Don't worry. I've helped a number of *NY Times Bestselling Authors* and celebrity clients over the past decade, including Tony Robbins, Tim Ferriss, Darren Hardy (publisher of Success Magazine), Debbie Ford, Brendon Burchard, Brian Tracy, Harvey Mackay, Arielle Ford, John Assaraf, Dan Kennedy, and many more.

I'd like to share the same online marketing and promotions strategies that I used to help of these thought leaders because these same techniques will help you too.

I'll also introduce you to 5 "marketing machines" that can automate and make this entire process super fast and easy.

 *My Story...*

For me, it all began in tiny town called Eagle Lake, Minnesota. I grew up in a lower middle-class family, and I never had the means to go to college. But like you, I've always had big dreams.

When I was 14 years old, a neighbor loaned me an Apple II computer during Christmas vacation, which was an incredible gift for me. I was one of four kids, and my entire family lived off of my father's humble earnings as a barber. A new computer is something my family could never afford.

Knowing that my time with this precious device was limited, I took advantage of the opportunity. That weekend, I taught myself how to program my friend's computer. I was enthralled, captivated, and completely infatuated with the possibilities the instrument represented. I did little else than tinker with that computer all weekend. Eventually, my insatiable desire to master the computing world led me into a niche field that eventually became my ticket out of Eagle Lake and into California. I started writing video games.

I have always loved movies, entertainment, music, and video games. So, this transition was a natural progression for me. In fact, my first company, Digital Cafe, combined each of these passions in one place. Founded in 1989, Digital Cafe was one of the first interactive marketing agencies. Our specialty was making "promotional entertainment" products—little marketing movies, CD-ROMs, custom music, animations, video games, and screen savers for big brands.

It took me until my late 20s (and I busted my butt to get there) but eventually, my business partner and I picked up 20th Century Fox and Sony Entertainment as clients, and we started developing video games and screen savers to promote their movies.

Eventually, our clients asked us to come out to Los Angeles to meet with them. It was the middle of February, and trust me—getting a couple of Minnesota kids to come to sunny California wasn't hard to do! We were leaving behind blistering temperatures of 30 degrees below zero, and we were full of ideas about movie stars, glitz, and glamour. To get an image of who were at this stage in our lives, just imagine a couple of Northern hicks from the movie, *Fargo*, on their way to Hollywood for the first time. Our level of enthusiasm and excitement was off the charts.

The moment I got off the plane, I smelled flowers in February. I saw the intense violet Jacaranda trees blooming in the winter. I will never forget the smells, sights, sounds, and feelings of my first trip to California. The Avenue of the Stars, Sunset Strip, Kodak Theater, Mann Chinese Theater, Santa Monica Boulevard and Beverly Hills—these were landmark sites I had previously only seen on TV. I fell in love on that trip, and that's one of the reasons I live in Southern California today.

I don't know about you, but whenever I watch the Academy Awards, the Grammys and the Emmys... I used to imagine myself getting an Oscar, Grammy, or Emmy. How about you? Most everyone I know wants to be acknowledged and recognized for his or her good work, skills, talents, creativity, accomplishments, results, know-how, experience, and expertise.

But, at least for me, it's never been about the glamour of the award, the fame, or the money. I always just imagined myself giving my acceptance speech, waving to the camera and saying "hi, Mom." I wanted to feel like all my hard work and efforts had paid off, and I wanted to thank the people who mattered, who contributed, who got me there.

And then... I wanted to be able to leverage that fame to make an even bigger difference, to be able to contribute hundreds of thousands or millions of dollars to charities, people, and organizations that need help.

From the deepest fiber of my being, that is what inspires, drives, connects, and reconfirms my commitment to doing the hard work it takes to make a difference and be successful in this world. Although money and recognition feel nice in the moment—those benefits are mere byproducts of what really matters to me—impacting lives for the greater good.

Here's a short 2 minute video about me
http://0s4.com/r/MIKEK

Or scan this handy QR code to jump right to the YouTube video:

 *Your Juice*

What about you? What gets you juiced?

What lights you up? What drives you? What is your WHY? What inspires you to put forth the effort required to do your best every day? What's your passion or spark?

It's good to dream. It's good to get fully associated to the outcome you desire most. Feel it and taste it! That's the first step to making anything you can imagine, real.

Let's get practical. What if you could double, triple, or quintuple your value and what you get paid for your products and services *right now*? What if you were getting paid around the clock – selling your *knowledge* instead of your *time*? What if you were able to continually take home an extra $5,000, $10,000, $25,000, or more every month without having to trade time for money? What if you were able to be paid for your knowledge and products instead of for your time and services? *How would that feel?*

In contrast, how would it feel if you knew you were going to die with your message still inside you? What if you never allowed yourself to reach your full potential? What if you were never able to broadcast your message to the world?

How would it feel to never be acknowledged or rewarded for your true gifts? Imagine the frustration of not being able to take care of your family or friends at the level you want. Imagine never making a difference, of living small and not contributing fully.

Life Is Short

I have a confession to make. Something very dramatic happened to me a few months ago. It was scary, and I don't wish it on anyone, but when all was said and done, it reconnected me to my deepest mission and my "big why". If you've ever faced the worst thing imaginable—loss of everything, death of a loved one, or a death sentence of your own—you'll know what I'm talking about.

A couple months ago, I was diagnosed with cancer. At just 46 years old, all of my dreams were shattered in a single instant of bad news.

After an exam, my doctor informed me that I had a large malignant tumor growing inside me. For three long days, I didn't know if I should expect to live another month, for 90 days, or for a year. And even if I was expected to live, I had no idea how this could affect the quality of my life. I imagined the worst.

I have a *big* mission. I have a huge message, a huge dream that's still inside of me. And, I have a family who I cannot bear to think about leaving behind – a beautiful wife and incredible 10 year old son who still needs his daddy. I never thought I'd be "that guy" with cancer. I simply never thought it would happen to me.

I have to admit, it's been rough. As I write this, I am recovering from major surgery and I've been going through eight months of aggressive chemotherapy, radiation and a combination of complementary and alternative therapies, nutrition, supplementation, meditation and energy work.

For as many as ten days in a row, I was not able to get out of bed. On the bad days, I would walk around with my eyes closed just to conserve energy. Drinking a glass of cold water felt like I was swallowing broken glass.

The good news is—it looks like I'm going to be okay, and I think the worst is behind me. We were able to catch it before the cancer spread... which would have only given me a year or less to live.

I'm not telling you this for sympathy, pity, or mercy.

I'm sharing this with you because it reminded me that I have a lot to live for—my family, my young son and wife, my parents, my brothers and sisters, incredible friends and an incredibly supportive community. I also have a *big* dream that I still need to share with the world. I still have this vision that I can radically transform and change lives at a massive scale. My plan is to create one million successful entrepreneurs worldwide. I want to help create one million millionaires who can use my tools get their message and expertise out to the world

That's my legacy. That's what I want to leave behind. And, I'd like to create financial stability for my son and wife in the process. I want them to be supported if I'm not here.

So, if you are reading this book right now, I have a message for you. *You* are my purpose. *You* are my passion.

I choose you.

Your success is what I strive for. You are what juices me, what makes my life worthwhile. My dream for you is that you step into your purpose, your authentic voice, that you realize your potential, and that you share your expertise with the world. And, I *know* you can do this.

It's your time to shine; it's your time to be a star.

The Time Is Now

Right now, in this instant, we live in the greatest moment in human history.

There are over two billion connected computers and over six billion mobile connections in use worldwide. *And*, those numbers are expected to grow to 15 billion by 2015 – two Internet connected devices for every person on the planet. Right now, you can record a video on a smartphone and with the click of a button; you can communicate with nearly 85% of the human race, basically for free. What kind of power is that? Think about it!

The rules of distribution have changed—massively. That's an unbelievable opportunity for you and me. We're in control of the media. The big media giants are no longer in charge. Anyone and everyone can broadcast a message.

Today's smartphones have a built-in high-definition camera that's the equivalent of a portable TV studio in your hand. Press a button, broadcast all over the world. It's as simple as that. You. Everywhere. Now.

It's just as easy to distribute your message, also. You can publish videos on YouTube, where you can basically create your own TV channel.

Within 24 hours, you can have a book published and distributed on Amazon—for free! And with a little know-how, you can create a multi-media product, put it online, and start collecting money that same day.

When you combine this level of production simplicity and distribution reach with social media channels, there are no longer any barriers. There is no limit to the type of relationships you can build. At this point in time, it is possible to do business with virtually anyone on the planet.

To bring your message to life, all it takes is a tiny bit of effort, the right tools and the right kind of training.

The technological possibilities today are everywhere. The Internet, mobile apps, Amazon, Apple, mobile phones, tablets, blogs, podcasts, Membership Sites have all put the power of the media into the hands of the *people*—you and me. Big distribution is almost completely free and the "old ways" of distributing content that require someone else's permission are rapidly becoming obsolete, unprofitable, and irrelevant.

What's more? The opportunities in this market are huge. The corporate training and e-learning industry generates $33 billion per *year*, the eBook and book publishing industry is worth $27.94 billion, the personal growth market nets $10.5 billion, the mobile app market is worth

$17 billion, the coaching market pulls in $1.2 billion, and digital information product have more than doubled in the last five years.

Does that excite you? It blows my mind. There is *so* much opportunity right now to teach, share, and sell information. Feel inspired. You have the chance *right now* to change lives with *your message and knowledge.*

We believe the secrets that you'll discover in this short book are one of the easiest and fastest ways to grow to be a six-figure business. As a small business owner, entrepreneur, author, expert, consultant, or coach, it's possible to use the strategies in this book to build a sustainable business in as little as 18-36 months. Of course, it's up to you to take the action to get it done.

You must prepare yourself for the journey because the time is now. Your starting point isn't important: whether you are starting from square zero, or you've been in business for decades, this process is about reexamining and reinventing yourself. Take advantage of the incredible technology that exists right now and don't spare another moment.

So, how do you go about starting? What's the first step? There are almost too many possible avenues for content distribution available. Getting started can be overwhelming.

Your Expertise + Technology = A REAL Business

So how do you combine this technology with your know-how into a profitable business? It's not necessarily quick and easy. There is no "get-rich-fast" trick to make this work. The fundamentals of all quality businesses still exist in this new market—you still have to add real value, develop a strong base of customers, establish quality relationships, and operate with integrity.

Your simply using tried and true business tactics to maximize one of the fastest growing market forces in the world, and it can be done in five steps...

I've been building a refining this system for over a decade. I've customized it for hundreds of best-selling authors, experts, and authorities, but until now, the technology and distribution costs have made it exclusive to only those with big enough bank accounts or a significant level of notoriety. That's not the case anymore. Technology has opened the doors, and literally anyone with a passion behind his or her message can successfully master this system.

You don't have to be tech-savvy. You don't have to be a marketing wizard. You don't have to have a pedigree or a diploma from a fancy school. Lord knows, I barely even passed high school. Almost zero capital is required, you don't need any employees to make it work, there is a low level of risk, and it even works if you're terrified of being on camera, presenting on stage, or networking. There is absolutely nothing stopping you from starting immediately.

However, before you begin, there is one thing you must have in place. As I mentioned previously, there is one big word that is the cornerstone of your success. It is the one factor you've probably been missing. This is the cure to selling your knowledge instead of your time, multiplying your value by a factor of ten, becoming recession- and competition-proof and earning hands-free continuity income.

It's called a *platform*.

So, "What's a platform?" you ask? It's what you know, what you have to say, your special experience and expertise combined with who knows *you*. Who would pay to read your book? Who is willing to purchase your products? Who would pay just to hear you speak?

- Your connections & contacts
- Your list
- Your ability to get attention, create buzz

- Your products and services
- Your celebrity status
- It's your "CURRENCY" – it's true, unlimited wealth and it's leverage for life
- No bank, no economy can take it from you

You need it. Your clients need it.
Every single business needs it.
Every single person on the planet needs a platform and a system to get the word out.

And they'll *pay you a fortune* to build it for, or with them.

With a platform, you get paid what you are worth and deserve. With it, you're unstoppable. You're free.
And your platform doesn't have to be HUGE to be massively profitable or effective.

For example, in my experience a list of 10,000 names can easily earn you $1,000,000 per year and you can keep all the money because you're in control and you're in charge.

A platform gives you the ability to make a couple of phone calls - and with your leverage get on news, media, blogs or access JV (Joint Venture) partners promote and market your products and services. All of these resources are essentially "lending" you their platform in exchange for your knowledge. It's a win-win-win!

A platform is TRUE WEALTH; it's LEVERAGE FOR LIFE that can pay you continuity income for life.

Let me give you a few examples...

A restaurant owner with no customers is going broke. It's because he's got no platform. If he did, he could send an email, mobile text message, tweet, Facebook message or post a video on YouTube and fill the restaurant in a couple hours, every day, for the rest of the week and month and probably for years to come.

A struggling author loves her book and really believes her message will change the world. But she's doesn't have a platform. If she did...and even it were small, she could sell 2,000 to 5,000 books in a couple of weeks - enough to be a NY Times Bestselling Author (yes, really—this can happen, heck, it DID happen to a whole bunch of my friends and clients—and it can happen to you too)

A consultant is struggling to trade dollars for hours. Again, no platform. If he had one, he would have a bunch of prospective clients on a waiting list. At that point, fees aren't even an issue—people don't even bat an eye when you quote 5- and 6-figure numbers for consulting or speaking.

...and it is all because of PLATFORM.

OH...and here is the really cool thing.

It used to be that to create a platform, you'd need an agent, a publisher, a full-time publicist (and maybe even a hair-stylist :) – plus, years and years of exposure to get a platform.

Building a platform is about connecting your list of prospects and customers with your know-how and unique gifts. It's your influence, your connections, and your reach. To make this all work, you first need to know what you are selling and to whom.

What is your unique story? How can you share it with the world in an original, compelling, and enthusiastic way?

Once you have that, the steps that follow will ensure that your efforts to build a profitable business are laser-focused, meaningful and substantive.

 5 Steps to Launching Your Author Expert Marketing Machines Platform

There are 5 P's in this process:

1. Position
2. Publish
3. Product
4. Promote
5. Profit

Step 1: Position

To start building a powerful, enduring, profitable platform, you have to become the number one person in your niche. You need to position yourself as the "go to" person for your area of expertise. You need to be the big fish in town, the star of your domain.

It's really not that hard.

The key is to first get associated to your "why". Know what makes you passionate about your area of expertise and exert that energy into everything you do. Then, create a story around your background that encompasses your expertise and your vision. Create a relationship with your audience and establish your credibility among the people with that scope. Your outcome is to get people to know you, but more than that—you want them to trust you.

Here's why this is so important.

Once you have achieved a level of trust and respect in your chosen subject, you can begin charging more money for your time, products, and services. In fact, with some prestige and a known reputation, you will likely have the ability to charge two times, five times, or even ten times more money for *everything* you offer. Plus, once enough people know you and demand your work, the media will start coming to *you*. Your products and services can literally be identical to that of your competitors—but your *platform, your story* increases your value.

And, once that happens, you can leverage it to generate even more business, more money, and more attention. This becomes a powerful cycle and an unstoppable force of momentum.

Maybe you already understand this; everything you need to "know" to position yourself is already inside you right now. You already have what it takes to showcase yourself as *the* expert in a topic about which you are passionate and knowledgeable. Perhaps you've taken your inherent strengths for granted, perhaps you don't know how much you really know relative to others, or perhaps you're just afraid to put yourself out there.

The point is—your talent is waiting untapped. All you have to do is uncover, define, and translate that gift into something tangible others can benefit from. Then, position yourself as the best... because you are.

Step 2: Publish

The second "P" in building your unstoppable platform is *publishing*. You need to publish something, to put your work into black and white, tangible text or get your message distributed online in a meaningful way.

And no, this doesn't mean you have to write a whole book.

Now, in the old days, you needed permission to publish. You had to grab the attention of an agent, who had to deem your work worthy enough to send out to publishers, who then weighed your manuscript against hundreds of others to determine which would potentially make *them* the most money. You had to trust the judgment of others—who are more than likely *not* experts in your field to decide whether or not your book would ever make it in front of your audience.

It used to take two years to complete this process. By the time a book finally made it into print, the passionate need for content leading to its inception was nearly outdated. Once in print, you had to either know someone or patiently persist in your campaign to get the attention of the media. It used to take months or even years to get publicity on television, the radio, newspapers, or magazines.

The big media giants were the gatekeepers who determined what would go to market for all to see and what wouldn't. Distribution used to be king, and those in creative fields were at the mercy of the big companies who controlled it. Authors, musicians, and artists were often paid a paltry sum relative to the success of their works. It was not uncommon for content providers to be paid less than a dollar per sale after the distributor took out all of their expenses.

Think about the movie stars of the 60's, 70's, 80's, and 90's who are now broke and selling shoes for a living. Yes— some squandered their money and made poor choices, but none of them were paid for their efforts in entirety, and many were cheated out of their right to wealth by shady accounting schemes. They all had to rely on a "middle man" of some sort to take their art and put it into the world for them. They didn't control the KING of platform: *distribution.*

The Internet has changed all of that. Today, distribution is practically free. It's democratic.

There is no longer the need to deal with a greedy "middle man." All you need is an index finger and a laptop, and you have access to 88% of the entire human race.

Publishing used to a huge barrier. It used to be available only to a lucky few, but in today's world, publishing is the easiest step of this entire process. You just have to put what you have out there and understand how to "position" yourself and tell your story in a way that's meaningful to your audience.

We'll get to the "secret" to that shortly.

Then, once you're a published author, you will likely suddenly become worth two to ten times more money... which translates into more media attention, more speaking gigs, more opportunities to grow even more.

The best part of the publishing world today is that you get paid immediately too. You can sell your work one piece at a time and get paid the moment something sells. You don't have to juggle inventory. There is literally nothing to lose if your content doesn't sell right away, or at all, but if it does sell—you get to reap the rewards, all of them. You don't have to wait for anyone or anything. You're in charge. You're in control. This is a beautiful thing.

 *Step 3: Product*

Regardless of your personal or professional niche, people will pay you for the knowledge you bring to the table. You cannot take this for granted or sell yourself short. You need to package and sell your information. You need a product.

Maybe you're saying, "But, I'm in the service business," "I'm a professional consultant," "I'm a psychiatrist, photographer, musician, artist, etc."

Let me say this again. It doesn't matter what industry you specialize in, there is a set of principles, keys, and practices that surround it. And, someone, somewhere is hungry for that information. You just have to get the concepts out of your head and into a tangible format others can master.

Turning your ideas into tangible products is the difference between trading time for money and trading time for value. This is your ticket to freedom and a life with no financial ceiling.

Your product will be a primary source of income and an opportunity to create even more products and services that will become upsells in the future. Most importantly, the product will be a way to go deeper with your audience, to help them gain better access to your expertise, and to walk through the blueprint that your customers need to solve their problems.

Suddenly your local "service business" has the potential to become an international business. Your art could become a household name. You can sell to anyone, anywhere, anytime... on autopilot.

If you are a speaker (or want to be), you now have something to offer people after your presentation. This is something you can offer to all of your existing customers as well as those you have not met. You can generate sales both in person and online.

Ideally, you want a product that can be sold for $50-$1,000 or more. By the way, I can help you put it together. I have a simple 5-step process for turning your ideas into products that anyone can do. This combined with a one-page site that collects money and automatically delivers your products to any Internet-connected device is a win-win-win system.

There is no inventory and no physical product. You can sell as many products as you want, and *you* get to keep all the money.

Turning your idea into a product is the best new investment opportunity since the Internet was invented.

To get started, you need to decide *what* you will publish and produce. What are the topics in which you are already an expert? What do you know a lot about? Do you have any existing work already in print? Survey your audience— what do they want to know more about?

Soon, I'll guide you through a process that will unlock your knowledge and know-how in a way that can be easily turned into powerful content that can be easily turned into a book or product.

Next, start with what you know, but have the bigger picture in perspective. Design an easy path for your customers to pay you by thinking about the order in which your information would unfold. Once they finish your first book, what product will they crave next? Then, what will they want after that? And after that?

There's a formula and a process for all of this.

The more proactive you can be about anticipating your audience's needs, the more value you'll provide and the more prolific your business model will become. There is no end to how much you can produce and consequently, how much profit you can generate.

You can create another product, a coaching program, online events, and/or live events. All of these pieces work together to create a valuable experience that accentuates your message and reinforces your client's ability to follow through and take action.

But, here's a quick piece of advice—choose one topic, establish your credibility in that area, and stick with it. Don't try to write and speak about any additional topic until you've mastered the first one. Jumping around from one topic to another will lose people. Instead, your goal is to create a solid reputation in one subject matter. This will reinforce your credibility and therefore, your results.

Once you've created a suite of products, you can then use them in creative and meaningful ways to entice and support your customers. Lead your clients through your content by upselling them into something else at the close of each product. This supports them... *and you.* This is a simple formula for ongoing success. Provide value and upsell by showing customers the next step in your journey. Provide more value. Repeat the process. Again. And again. And again.

Remember—your credibility is paramount. If you lose that, you lose everything.

Credibility is built by constantly and consistently showing irrefutable proof that your knowledge, your products and services produce results. Capturing testimonials, photos and videos that show your clients and customers that your products work does this.

If you visit www.AuthorExpertMarketingMachines.com and watch video #3 in the free video training series, you'll see an example of this "formula" at work. This video shows real customers that have produced results with my products and services.

Step 4: Promote

So, now you have a platform, you've positioned yourself as an expert in your field, you've published your work, and you have at least one product that you're able to sell instead of your time. Next step?

It's all about getting the word out there.

You need marketing. Always be marketing. And it's easy when you know the simple secrets to making it happen.

You wouldn't believe how many times I speak with small business owners, entrepreneurs, authors, experts, speakers, consultants, and coaches who get some attention, maybe show up on TV or the radio, and have nothing to sell and no way to capture names to build a list.

Back when Oprah was featuring authors on her show, there were literally hundreds of authors who got on the program, but had nothing to sell. They got their shot and didn't make any money—except maybe seeing a spike in book sales for a day or two. They never built a list. They didn't have a complete platform.

Don't be that person. That's why promotion is Step 4 and not Step 1. If you've done all of the above, you will be ready once you have the media's attention.

Build a list.

Your list is your currency. It's your pathway to power and *freedom* from selling your time. With a list, you can create deals, establish joint venture partnerships, get bigger publishing deals with industry players, and build momentum. Having a list turns the tables around. Big publishers will come to *you*, begging *you* to work with them because you have access to hungry prospects and customers who want what you have, not the other way around.

When you have both a list and a product, you have the equivalent of a printing press that legally prints money on demand.

This is a self-sufficient system that puts you in the driver's seat. Your list is your community. They are people who want your message and who will pay you for your products.

Darren Hardy, the publisher of *Success* magazine, built a list of over 200,000 names and phone numbers in only a year. Want to know how much a list that big is worth? Let me put it to you this way, after sending just *four* emails, Darren earned over $250,000 four times in a row! Four emails, $1,000,000.

But, you don't even need that many people to profit. My companies grossed over $13 million a year two years in a row with a list of fewer than 120,000 names. That's over $1,000,000 for every 10,000 names in the list.

To me, that's the magic number – when money isn't an issue anymore. 10,000 names with a product and a series of "Marketing Machines" that are doing the work for you.

When you have a list, you have more than one opportunity to sell. You have an ongoing relationship with people who will potentially buy multiple times from you.

To start building your list, focus on capturing leads. Give people a reason to give you their email address by providing value upfront in the form of free content. Then, test your offers in the system. Find out what people respond to. Then, do more of that.

Later in our free video series, I explain how all of this works and share with you tools that automate this entire process.

Now, I've saved the best step for last...

 *Step 5: Profit*

It's time to put money in your pocket *right now*.

My system shows you the top five ways to profit from your positioning, publishing, product, and promotion process. It shows you how to leverage your platform to get more attention and make real money as the authority, expert, and star that you already are.

The world just hasn't been introduced to you yet.

Note: If you decide to use the Author Expert Marketing Machine's system, we'll promote your book and your product to our list of nearly 250,000 and publish you in our online store.

This will literally kick-start your career and save you months or even years of having to do all the hard work yourself of building a platform from scratch. How much would that be worth to you?

Your Message:
What You Want to Be Known For

So, what's your core message that you want to share with to the world? And, why is this important to you? This is a very personal process so take some time to think it through. You will need to determine your "why" as well as your "what." Understanding why you do what you do is a key part of this process.

What are you known for?

What would you like to be known for?

If were to leave this world tomorrow, what would you want to be remembered for?

What would you like to create as a legacy?

Now take a moment to think about your story. What's your background?

What's your area of expertise?

How did you get from where you first started to where you are today?

What were the lows, the highs and the challenges you had to overcome along the way?

What advice would you give someone who was just starting out? Why?

The ultimate purpose of crafting your narrative is to help your audience identify with you and understand what you stand for. You may do something that thousands of other experts do, but if you have a unique story that allows people to get to know you, they will begin to like and trust you. This creates an emotional connection and instantly differentiates you from others in your field.

While you may have elements of your life and story that are entirely unique, it is important to become aware of the parts of your story that are *like* those of your audience. What will help them identify with you? What makes you more like them? It's simple: if you find these common story elements, your audience will like you because you are just like them. And if you build in aspects that make you trustworthy, they will trust you. Again, forming trust is the crucial first step that people need in order to embark on a journey with you.

So, ultimately... what's your story? What's the niche you want to star in? Why?

The Keys to the Kingdom:
How to Automatically Manifest Your Perfect Customer that Pays You Over and Over Again and How to Find Your Authentic Voice

It's time to give you the keys to the kingdom.

I'm going to get a little philosophical with you now, maybe even a bit spiritual. But I'm going to transform you into an incredible marketer with a 3-minute exercise. And if you're already a good marketer, I'm going to show you how to attract, influence, and deeply connect with your ideal customer.

And if you're terrified of being on camera or on stage and can't imagine yourself writing a book, then prepare yourself for a complete personal transformation.

Have you ever been afraid to fully share your authentic self publicly? Most people are.

However, it's the most powerful way to create a deep connection... Your authenticity resonates with people, and that's what hooks them. That's what makes them want more of anything you offer.

RESONATE

Verb:
1. *Produce or be filled with a deep, full, reverberating sound.*
2. *Evoke or suggest images, memories, and emotions.*

This is a spiritually based principle, and it's as old as time. But, the truth is, I know this works because I've helped thousands of people unlock their deepest fears about being able to speak or present on video or stage in minutes. I've seen their transformation from putting on a performance to coming from their core... and this switch makes all the difference. The secret is to connect from a place in you that's real, authentic, and raw. Coming from this place will attract your perfect customer to you almost as if it were magic.

Note: Your BS meter may be going off right now. I promise—you will be agreeing with me soon. This works.

If you look back 10,000 years ago or so, early religions and mystical traditions were passed on orally. There were no printing presses and no easy distribution methods. All information was passed on through stories. Young people were taught by memorizing stories.

Here's how it works. The human brain organizes facts as stories very efficiently. That's why stories about characters and people are easy to remember.

Look at the power of Christianity. The story of Jesus has radically affected billions of people for thousands of years. How? Jesus' disciples and followers had great content (like the son of God resurrecting from the dead). They told stories about the power of forgiveness, love, and transformation that resonated with an audience.

Fast-forward about 20 centuries. Many consider Steve Jobs to have been the greatest CEO storyteller in the world. It's no accident that Apple became the most valuable company in the world—largely because Steve was able to captivate hundreds of millions of people with stories of what's possible with Apple's products. His stories created massive demand for iPods, iPhones, iPads, and every one of Apple's latest gadgets.

Thanks to Steve and other technological wizards, you don't have to tell your story to one person at a time; you have the power to share your story with the entire connected planet simply by pressing a button. As I said before, you can communicate with nearly the entire human race through a mobile phone, tablet, desktop, or laptop computer.

Think about it. You have more reach now than any person who ever lived less than a century ago!

Let me show you how to connect with authenticity, to resonate with an audience, and to magically attract your perfect customer into your business or your life. This will also make it profoundly easy to write books and create profitable products. And, as a bonus—this exercise will help make you comfortable on camera or on stage too.

Sound impossible? Well, let's see...

The Best Customer Ever

This exercise is called, "The Best Customer Ever." I want you to describe the best customer or client you've ever had.

At www.AuthorExpertMarketingMachines.com, there's a free step-by-step video that guides you through this process in case you're an "immersive learner" like me. Just "opt-in" and you'll get the printable, downloadable "cheat sheet" companion to the video.

Who is someone who paid you for your products or services? Think of someone you loved working with. This is a person who took your advice, used your product or service, and got results. They happily paid you (and they keep coming back to you for more). They refer more customers to you, and they give you great testimonials. They're enthusiastic, warm, and happy. Best of all, if you had ten, 100 or 10,000 duplicates of this customer forever, your job would be easy and joyful.

All you have to do is attract more people who are like your ideal customer and you're set.

Write down a description of your ideal customer in as much detail as possible. (Note: If you're just starting out and don't have a business yet, then I want you to *imagine* your perfect customer.)

I'll give you an example. My ideal customer's name is Sue. She's 65 years old, but energetically, she's more like 30. Sue lives in Canada and is a pediatric anesthesiologist. Sue is divorced, has two children, Christopher and Lisa. Sue's biggest fear is that after 35 years of being a doctor, she'll never achieve her dream retirement.

Her greatest dream is help others live a rich and fulfilling life while traveling around the world... without any financial worries.

That sounds good to me, how about you?

What I like most about Sue is that she is eager, enthusiastic, filled with life, and absolutely passionate about helping other people. The reason I enjoy working with Sue is because she makes a commitment, executes a plan, and gets stuff done.

When Sue started coaching with me, she was afraid she couldn't turn her dream into a book or product. However, after only a single consulting session, Sue got clear on her message, her offer, and her product. She created total clarity on what she really wants.

The next day, Sue down in my video studio and told her story with clarity, passion, and vision. In as little as six months, she'll not only be ready to leave her job and have her book and product finished, but she'll be traveling the world, living her ultimate retirement dream while making money teaching others how to do the same.

The greatest wish that I have for Sue is that she'll sell 10,000 copies of her book and be living in dozens of different countries with hundreds or thousands of customers who she can coach in the next year—while making money, feeling purposeful, living fully, and impacting people who resonate with her message and mission.

Done. When you follow this process, you'll attract your ideal customer just like Sue.

Got it?

Exercise:

Step 1: Describe the best customer or client you've ever had (and if you're just starting out and don't have a business, then IMAGINE your perfect customer):

- Someone who paid you for your products or services.
- Someone you loved or love working with.

- Someone who took your advice, used your product or service.
- Someone who got results.
- Someone who happily paid you and kept coming back (or will continue to keep coming back).
- Someone who has, and will, refer more customers to you and give you great testimonials.
- Someone who's enthusiastic, warm and happy.

Go ahead, write in this book – it'll be FUN! :)

_____

_____

_____

_____

_____

_____

_____

_____

_____

_____

Step 2: Now, do the following (this is really easy!):

Hold your phone camera up with your left hand. Press the record button. Smile and put your right hand on your heart. Take a deep breath in, exhale into your heart (breathe nose-to-heart and back again, imagining the path of your breath following a circle).

Now, think about the best customer you've ever had.

Visualize them standing in front of your camera right now. Smile. Look into the camera and describe her or him. Say hi – say their name. Tell them who their children are. Have a full conversation. Feel them fully, with gratitude and love. Then, look into the camera and *think* about that person while you tell me a story about how you transformed their life or business with your products and services with *passion, enthusiasm, and gratitude.*

I want you to get emotional. This is not a thinking exercise; it's a *feeling* exercise.

So take a moment and record your video.

I can guarantee you, when you do this, you'll never feel or be nervous again – whether you do this on a stage in front of 5, 50 or 50,000 people or on a camera because you're OUT OF YOUR HEAD and IN YOUR HEART.

When you speak from a place of service, love and caring, it's impossible to be nervous. You're not worried about you and what other people think about you. You're focused on someone else.

This is the key. The secret to great marketing.

Speak to the one, don't think, *FEEL*. **RESONATE**.

How did it go?

From this point forward, whenever you make a marketing video, craft an email, create a blog post, or write your book, you're going to speak and write to your perfect customer.

Speak to THE ONE, Attract MANY

It's a little bit counter-intuitive, but if you speak to THE ONE, you will attract many just like them.

You see, if you speak or write to "everyone", you're speaking to no one. You're schizophrenic, and you'll attract crazy, cheap, rotten customers that will suck your life force and all the joy from your job and profession. I call them "psychic vampires" and they'll steal your soul and all the joy from your business, your life and purpose if you let them.

But when you speak to one, more like that person will be attracted to you, almost as if by magic. When you consistently speak directly to your one best customer, you will start attracting more people like him or her.

This is an exercise in manifestation. It is a spiritual act where the physical and the divine become one. Because after all, we *are* all one, right?

You Can Do This!

Now look at yourself in the mirror and repeat after me, "I CAN DO THIS!"

You can.

Want proof? Several years ago, we sold $9.1 million in products in one week during a product promotion. Six months later, we sold $7.1 million in a single week; $3.1 million was sold in a single day on a live internet video broadcast.

Would you like to know how I did it?

At an event, I met a young guy who was what I considered to be our "ideal customer" because he implemented and made money in a few hours. His name is "Fireman" Mike Lemoine. I wrote and read my next script to the camera as if I were speaking directly to "Fireman Mike".

Since then, Fireman Mike has become one of our star customers. *And, we've attracted more like him.*

After just a couple of years, Mike's on track to have a seven-figure year income! Other customers who are "like" Fireman Mike that we attracted during that promotion include Johnny Schrunk, Jimmy Harding, Eric Kurit, and Jody Underhill. They all have similar energy, personalities, values, and drive.

All have built huge platforms—and most are closing in on seven-figure years with our tools and resources. They've built businesses, coaching, and speaking platforms. Most of them built six-figure businesses just a few months after they started working with us.

Less than one year later, I was holding a live event, and I realized we had only about 15 percent women in our audience. I was appalled because I know that the fastest way to create a peaceful, fast-growing, conscious economy and planet is to empower women entrepreneurs. On stage that day, I declared (not having any idea how I'd do it) that we would have 35 percent women in the room at the next event.

During my next promotion, I read my script to the camera to a new customer I had just met at my event. Her name was Susan. She was *real* and heartfelt—someone who represented the kind of woman I wanted to attract as a customer. I knew how old she was, her marital status, her hopes, dreams, her fears and worries. I knew she had a son who was 8 years old and knew what he liked, and knew what she wanted in life—to give back, make a difference and make lots of money to be free. I could imagine her standing in front of me – what she wore and I even remembered what her perfume smelled like. I made her real. I spoke only to her.

When I finished my video, my message was softer, more heartfelt, and more genuine. It was more *real.* My message became attractive to women – because I spoke to one.

Guess what? Our sales to women nearly doubled from 14 percent to 27 percent. Almost 35 percent of the audience at our next live event was women – entrepreneurs who were very similar to Susan. What's more – and this still blows me away– our high-end mastermind and coaching program is now comprised of more than 50 percent women – and those customers pay us $25,000 per year for this coaching program. I have a dozen people in my high-end 1:1 coaching program that costs $125,000 per year. All of this happened because I practiced this exercise before making my marketing materials.

More recently, we attracted a new wonderful customer named Kristen who was attending that next event. She's a widowed mother of four, spunky as heck, and she earned over $90,000 in three weeks after using one of our systems. What's the best part? She spent only five hours setting up her "Marketing Machines". I don't know about you, but that's the kind of success story I want to share.

This is the power of "The Perfect Customer" exercise. It works for any business, anywhere in the world. I promise you, this is the most significant marketing and training exercise I've ever learned or taught.

But instead of it taking you 25 years to figure this out on your own like it did me, you can use it right now.

A Profound Secret

Resonating with your audience is the ultimate secret to really helping people with your message.

You see, people are like crystal wine glasses. When one vibrates, so do the others. The more raw, real, and authentic your message and stories, the deeper the connection will be. You'll magically attract *more* ideal customers. Your message will spread like crazy. This is what will make you go viral.

People appreciate that which makes them feel. There is so much clutter and noise in the world already. But, when you say something real, something of value, something that comes from that place deep inside you that's just being... you, it stands out. People are craving that type of connection in this noisy world. We're tired of being talked at, performed for, and sold to. At the end of the day, we just want authenticity. We just want to know what is honest, solid, and real.

Here's the bottom line—you've got to let your guard down...even if you're scared. You can't hold back. In order to resonate with people, you need to open up and find a grounded space where you are genuinely present and completely candid.

I was terrified to tell you about my cancer. I've been terrified to show you my deepest self, my spiritual self. But I chose to find the strength and courage to be completely raw and real with you.

In a way, I had nothing to lose. But then, I realized that I had everything to lose by not sharing my deepest light and my soul with you. In doing so, you and I have a deeper connection right now.

And I believe... no, I *know* it's had a profound shift on the quality of the relationship I have with you right now even if we've never met in person. I also know that if that level of authenticity and rawness offends or pushes you away, then I am not the right person to help you. And I'm ok with that. Great marketing attracts the right people and repels the pests.

This is the deepest and most profound marketing secret I can give you. I have to tell you—seven multi-million-dollar product promotions in a row didn't happen by accident.

I'm not saying this to you to boast. I'm saying this because I've spent 25 years of my life trying to learn the secret to marketing, and it was staring at me in the face the whole time.

So, don't resist the truth. Don't hold back. Be yourself... *your full, true self.* This is the path to your success.

I'd like to share another marketing secret with you. How would you like one more short, simple exercise that will position and turn you into an instant expert and authority? It will unlock knowledge you probably didn't even exist inside you – and you'll quickly find out you have an entire book and an entire product that's already inside you, just waiting to break free.

All you need is the tool to unlock it and I'm going to give it to you right now.

Are you game?

The 10x10x4 Formula:

A Simple Automated System to Authentically Connect to Your Ideal Customers All Over the Web

I was recently featured in *Success Magazine* and taught this process on a CD and in an article. By the way, that magazine article is an example of the power of "Platform"—being featured in that magazine is something that can never be taken away from me and provided continual credibility for the rest of my career. I want to give you a tool that will give you access to the mainstream media and much more right now.

By the way – there's a companion video that goes through this process step-by-step at www.AuthorExpertMarketingMachines.com in case you're an "immersive learner" like me.

This formula is based on something I've been teaching for years. When you combine the "perfect customer" exercise with this, it will instantly unlock knowledge inside that you probably didn't even know was there. This is quality information you already possess that can position you as the #1 "go-to" person in your niche. You can use it to create your first book or product in record time.

It's called the "10x10x4 Formula." You are going to start by creating a list of FAQs and SAQs.

FAQs are frequently asked questions that you get all the time.

For example, here are some I get:

- "What kind of video camera should I use?"
- "How long should an online video be?"
- "What should I wear when I'm on camera?"

These are questions people might ask you when they want to learn more about your area of knowledge or expertise. Note: They are not questions specific to the details surrounding your product or service. The goal in answering these questions is to educate, not to sell.

SAQs are "should ask" questions. These are the questions you *wish* people would ask you. It's the little nuances of your niche, the things you may have spent 5, 10, or even 30 years studying and refining. It's the type of things others outside your field don't know they don't know. This knowledge has come to you after thousands of hours of hard work, trial and error, and working in the trenches.

You've been sharing the same information over and over again—and if you could just broadcast it to the world quickly and easily, people would just come to you—already knowing they want to work with you or buy your products and services!

Here are a couple examples of great SAQ questions:

- "What's the best advice I can give someone starting out who wants to quickly and inexpensively make the best marketing content?"
- "Why is it a myth that you'll need expensive equipment to make powerful marketing videos?"

The biggest difference between FAQs and SAQs is that when people hear your response to an SAQ, they will be captivated by your knowledge, know-how, and wisdom. They'll be transfixed by your expertise and realize they couldn't possibly do whatever you offer on their own.

As a result, they'll quickly realize you're the answer to their problem or challenge. SAQs automatically position you as a leader and expert, and all humans are attracted to that. Plus, because the answers are unique to you and your expertise, you will instantly create a competitive gap between your stuff and someone else's.

Exercise:

Here's what I want you to do. Take a moment now and write down as many FAQs and SAQs as you can in three minutes. Timing yourself while you do this will help the ideas flow through you more rapidly. It takes the filter off and enables you to write more naturally.

If you write down five questions in three minutes, you'll have 100 questions in only an hour. If you are able to come up with ten, then you'll have 200. If you do 15, you'll have 300!

FAQs (Frequently Asked) SAQs (Should Ask)

_____   _____

_____   _____

_____   _____

_____   _____

_____   _____

_____   _____

_____   _____

_____   _____

_____   _____

_____   _____

_____   _____

_____   _____

_____   _____

_____   _____

_____   _____

_____   _____

_____   _____

_____   _____

_____   _____

Once you've finished writing down your questions, record yourself answering each question on video. (Again, be sure to speak directly your ideal customer.)

A couple of notes about this process. First, make sure the questions and answers are true to your story. Remember, the content you deliver should be congruent with your personal narrative. Next, do not create misleading videos. Make sure you answer specific questions and fully address a given topic. Don't be vague and try to cover too much territory in a single video.

Lastly, you're educating, not selling. Give enough information for people to take the next step. Make sure you reveal enough information for people to begin to know, like, and trust you. Remember, your job is to establish your expertise and make people interested in the content you have to offer.

If you pitch them too early or make these videos all about you, you're going to turn people off. Unless you're really a goof, you wouldn't ask a woman to marry you on the first date, would you? Well, then, don't make a move that's offensive until you have permission first (and that's discussed in the fifth "P" – Profit).

Now, this is the cool part.

If all you did was record your answers to your questions and put them online, you'd have 100-300 marketing videos that would position you as an instant expert and authority on your topic or niche.

Then, if you transcribe the videos and follow my simple publishing process, you'll have enough content for a book!

If you want to go even deeper and follow my simple product creation process, you'll have a product you can sell for $100-1,000 in less than a week. You'll be making money while you sleep.

Are you getting the power of this process?

Can you see how combining the right position with the right published work and product can generate real profit?

Do you see how identifying your perfect customer and resonating with your audience yields exponential benefits? And, if you combine all of that with this simple marketing formula, you can pull it all off in a remarkably short amount of time?

Are you getting how opportune the time is now to take advantage of this business model?

Everything you need to be positioned, published, productized, promoted and profiting is inside you right now.

My goal here isn't to overwhelm you. I just want to give you a taste of the incredible knowledge and power that you already have inside you. With the right process and coaching, you have the ability to turn that into incredibly valuable material that will make you shine.

I can help you make all this happen.

The Secret to Selling Millions of Dollars of Products in Hours, Days or Weeks

How to Deeply Connect with Your "Perfect Customer" and Create Deep Desire for You, Your Products or Services that Cause Prospects to Buy NOW

What I'm about to share with you works for any business, anywhere in the world. It doesn't matter if you're selling products or services. You can be a small business owner, consultant, coach, author, expert, speaker or manufacturer. It doesn't matter what language you or your customers speak. This is a universal principle that's based on a concept that's over 10,000 years old – as old as the written word.

Growing up, I dreamed of making a million dollars. I really thought that once I will hit that magic number, my life would suddenly change.

So for the next 25 years, I searched, I studied and tried to find the secret to making millions (or even "just" a million). It was my quest. Strangely, that magic million dollars always eluded me. That's because I was focused on the wrong thing. It was about how can I make $1 million versus how can I create massive value and serve someone in such a way that they would be willing to pay me $1,000, $5,000, $10,000 or even $100,000 for a product or service.

My first product was the "Internet infomercial Toolkit".

For years, I studied what is known as "direct response marketing" not knowing what it was. I never knew what marketing really was – but I loved getting "junk mail" and signed up to receive anything that a company would mail me. That meant I had baskets of junk mail coming to my home and I would watch those half-hour infomercials and be amazed when I see someone like Ron Popeil talk on TV.

At state fairs, I would stop and watch pitchman as they expertly convinced a large group of busy people to buy their knives, gadgets, or whatever newfangled doodad would grab their attention. Those traveling salesmen mesmerized me.

I watched. I studied. I worked for over 20 years marketing and creating products for other people – but I always got paid for my time, not my value. I wasn't making products for ME. I was a hired gun.

There's no way you can make a million dollars working for someone else unless you're willing to live cheaply, save everything you can and be willing to forego lots of pleasures.

That isn't me. Until recently, I never saved a dime – always spending it on equipment, courses, live events, personal development and training...building the experience that would help me EXPLODE into the marketplace.

It wasn't until I started producing my own live events that the "million dollar secret" appeared in front of me. From that point, within six months, my company started to sell millions of dollars worth of our products and services.

What I'm about to share with you next to brag or impress you, but to impress upon you that I believe I figured out the secret and the solution to making millions. What I am about to share with you is my entire marketing model and the reason why I achieved success so many times in a row consistently.

In less than three years, I have created and launched and earned multiple millions of dollars in under a week – eight times in a row. The largest product launch earned over $9.1 million in a single week. In fact, when opened our online shopping cart and officially started taking orders, we earned $1 million in only 43 minutes. After just one hour and 14 minutes, we earned $2 million.

During a live direct to camera Internet "live webcast", I sold over $3.1 million worth of products in one day.

This didn't happen by accident. I followed a precise formula. After doing it eight times, it isn't in accident. It's not luck and I believe that anyone can do it if you have the right mixture of a great product, a great offer, and when you carefully mix this super special secret ingredient together.

So what is the special secret ingredient? It's simple, just add *stories of transformation.*

Human beings are "story receptors". Before there was a written language, there were stories. People communicated using stories. They sat around fires and shared wisdom and history through stories. Our brains remember things best when they are told in a story format. There is a formula to a great story.

I won't get into this in crazy detail, but the famous author, Joseph Campbell studied story structure and built a structure he called the "monomyth" – the "heroes journey". You can read more about it in the fantastic WikiPedia article here http://en.wikipedia.org/wiki/Monomyth.

Virtually every great story from Jesus Christ, Moses, Mohammed and Buddha follow the monomyth and virtually every culture's sacred and holy works follow this basic pattern.

When I began this chapter – I shared with you a basic story of transformation. It's about me and my quest was to make a million dollars. I struggled for years and went on a lifelong quest searching for the "gift" or the secret. After decades of failures, I finally found that "gift" or secret and upon learning and using that gift, realized it wasn't the MONEY I was searching for, but becoming valuable and helping other people achieve a personal or professional transformation with my products and services and sharing their stories of transformation with other people.

Only then did I make the money... It wasn't the money I was after all along, it was the personal transformation of helping other people transform!

From a marketing perspective, when you use this basic "formula" – the monomyth, it's immediately recognizable to the viewer or reader and so it engenders trust. For you, that means instant rapport – and because the human brain loves STORY so much, the viewer, listener or reader will continue through to the end and that's where you make the sale!

In a monomyth, the hero begins in the ordinary world, and receives a call to enter an unknown world of strange powers and events. The hero who accepts the call to enter this strange world must face tasks and trials, either alone or with assistance. In the most intense versions of the narrative, the hero must survive a severe challenge, often with help. If the hero survives, he may achieve a great gift or "boon." The hero must then decide whether to return to the ordinary world with this boon. If the hero does decide to return, he or she often faces challenges on the return journey. If the hero returns successfully, the boon or gift may be used to improve the world.

Here's a diagram of "The Hero's Journey" taken from the WikiPedia article mentioned above.

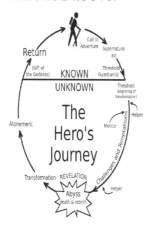

You, your products or services (or combination of all of them) represent the "helper" and "mentor" that cause the revelation and transformation in your customers. They are drawn to you because you are able to identify and communicate their pain in a way that they trust and believe you have the answer and solution on a personal level.

This is marketing. Plain and simple.

In our business, we are constantly on the search for a special type of customer. This is someone who rapidly implements our products and services and uses them and achieves some kind of result. The result is very important, they must be able to show or share some form of irrefutable proof that they actually use the product and something significant happened in their life as a result of this.

The kind of results were looking for include:

- making money
- quitting their job and starting a new business
- hiring employees
- saving a business from closing
- becoming a number one best-selling author
- receiving some kind of recognition or reward
- saving theirs or someone else's life
- getting national or local press or media attention
- doubling their income in 30 to 90 days
- being on track to earning six figures per month
- or being on the fast track to earning $1 million in a single year

In our business, we require that our customers show us some form of physical, irrefutable proof that they have achieved some kind of result in a certain period of time and that that result is repeatable and achievable.

In the bottom line is, I interview those people, find out who they are, what they did and how their life has been changed.

It's a transformational story that I'm after. I'm searching for their personal "hero's journey".

In our business, we identify and call customers who are fast implementers and on track to earning six figures with our tools and resources, "heroes". I often fly them out to our studio for an interview, share their videos online, put their stories in my books, and we often have them speak and present on our stage as a panelist or expert.

Here are some of our "heroes" and "all stars" at the "Digital Café" studios in San Diego, California

In short, I make them very visible and often, famous.

There is another level of transformational hero. Those who are on track or have earned $1 million or more within two years are called "All-Stars". Most of them began as heroes, they rapidly implemented, were able to share and show your beautiful proof of their success and they have another magical element to them.

They're leaders. And with a little bit of support, they can also become teachers. In fact, most do.

All-Stars are brought into my "inner circle". They are invited to come speak at our live events. I spend time teaching and training them on how to speak with authority and confidence. They get more attention in our marketing. And I invite and pay them to become teachers and trainers in our online courses.

In short, I give them a platform. And with that platform, they frequently triple or quintuple their income in a single year because they are legitimized and branded by my company and me.

So how can you do this for your business?

It's really quite easy, what you need and want to do is start a dialogue with your customers. There are many ways to reach out and bond with them and find transformational stories that you might not be aware of.

You can get some basic information from:

- surveys
- community feedback
- webinars and teleseminars
- direct mail and postcards
- contests and drawings
- emails they send to you!

I'm very direct when I search for success stories. Here's an example of a video that is requesting success stories from my customers. Feel free to model it. I'm just using a simple lead capture page that I built inside instant customer.

Here's one I made while I was at Times Square during Thanksgiving – shot from an iPhone:
http://0s4.com/r/PROOF1

And here's another one that I shot in my studio:
http://0s4.com/r/PROOF2

Notice the questions I ask – this is everything you need to capture EXCELLENT pre-qualifying candidates to feature in your marketing.

In case you don't have time to check out the pages, here are the questions I ask:

- What is your name?
- Where do you live?
- What do you currently do for a living?
- What type of business does you or your client have?
- What was life or business like before Instant Customer or Traffic Geyser?
- What specifically did you do with Instant Customer or Traffic Geyser?
- What specific results did you get with Instant Customer or Traffic Geyser?
- What does your client say (or a witness to YOUR SUCCESS) say about the change that Instant Customer or Traffic Geyser provided?
- Share something really interesting, WEIRD OR UNUSUAL about you that nobody knows about?

Note that the LAST question is actually the most important – because I find out if the candidate has CHARACTER. Some people will write something such as "I like music" which is BORING.

One of my FAVORITE candidates mentioned she kissed Mark Hamill (Luke Skywalker) when she was 15 years old because they used to live next to each other. I would up using that as a subject line in my next marketing email! Seriously, real life is stranger than fiction and you can't make this stuff up!

I require everyone to fill out the survey form AND submit a short video. I can tell in less than five seconds if the person is presentable, articulate, honest and likeable. No matter how good the story may seem, if they don't pass the "crazy eyes" test, I won't feature them.

By "crazy eyes" – you know what I mean. If they look like they have a pile of Mexican jumping beans bouncing around behind their eyes, they DEFINITELY don't pass the test ☺.

Next, I arrange interviews with the candidates that I feel have the highest probability of actually being successful. My assistant will arrange an interview using Skype video, GotoMeeting, or a Google hangout.

I record the entire conversation and video with ScreenFlow or Camtasia. These are software programs that run on Macintosh or PC computers. Both products cost less than $100 and are worth their weight in gold.

Here's a link to Camtasia – there's a 30-day free trial and it's available for both Windows PC and Macintosh:

http://0s4.com/r/CAM

Here's ScreenFlow – it's only available for the Macintosh but it's extremely powerful and easy to use:

http://0s4.com/r/SCREEN

Here are the basic questions that I ask every person that I interview:

- Who are you?
- Where are you from?
- What do you do for a living?
- What were the biggest challenges you have before you started using my product?
- How has your life changed since using my product?
- Can you show proof of the change that has occurred since using the product?
- What do other people, your spouse, your children, your friends say about the changes that have taken place in your life?
- What will your life be like now that these changes have occurred?
- What would you say to someone who is hesitant or on the fence or doesn't believe that this product will work for them?

I make a point of interviewing as many successful customers as possible. Without exception, these people a representative "avatars" of customers that invest in my products.

By avatar, that is a type of person – a specific combination of demographic and psychographic individual with their own worries, problems, life challenges, economic circumstances, and fears that must be overcome before they will become a customer.

Every transformational story is a tool and a resource that can overcome virtually every and every buying objection someone else just like them would have.

When these stories are told in a book, a video or a product launch sequence, the number of people who read watch or listen to them and buy will increase dramatically.

This is, by far, the most powerful secret and strategy aside from "the perfect customer exercise" that I shared with you earlier that will result in doubling, tripling or even quintupling the number of sales you will receive. (if you are reading this outside of my book, "Author Expert Marketing Machines", you can get it on Amazon.com or by visiting http://0s4.com/r/BOOKAE.

You don't have to be special for this to work for you, there's no magic. There's no complicated formula. The answer comes down to some really simple principles:

1. Become a servant to your customers and adopt the "servant" mentality and attitude
2. Get fully invested in the success of your customers when they use and implement your products and services
3. Imagine and then find the perfect story of

transformation that you want to share and tell with your prospects that will overcome their primary buying objections

4. Locate those successful customers. I promise, you already have them

5. Interview them and share their stories of transformation with your prospects

6. Feature and popularize your customers – it will draw more to you who want to feel and experience the same thing the "famous" ones are

7. People treat online video the same way they see people on TV – you're famous. They want to feel significant too.

If you want to watch in example of some stories of transformation, make sure you watch video number three, our "proof" video in this sequence:

www.AuthorExpertMarketingMachines.com.

You can also watch another "proof" video by visiting this page and watching the third video:

www.InstantCustomerRevolution.com.

To get started, find the success stories your clients and customers are already experiencing – watch the "request for proof" survey videos I shared with you above and check out the two web sites with proof videos for examples.

There are dozens of additional resources in the Author Expert Marketing Machines course on how to do this. I share and show how to do the interviews, what equipment to buy and use, and training on how to capture and edit those stories.

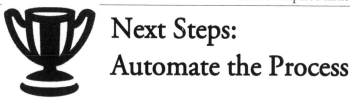

Next Steps:
Automate the Process

What if there was a tool that you could use to fill in the blanks, load up those short FAQ and SAQ videos we just made, press a button and bam—publish you and your content all over the web?

There is. It's called the "Instant Positioning Machine." We used this tool to help Harvey MacKay get his book, *Use Your Head to Get Your Foot in the Door* to a NY Times #4 Bestseller Status. We also used it to promote Tim Ferriss' book, *The Four-Hour Body*, Dan Kennedy's *No BS Wealth Attraction*, and Harvey Mackay's *MBA in a Day*. And, dozens of other authors and experts have used it too.

You can also use this to distribute your videos all over the web, to capture leads, to build your list, and to establish your platform.

We have a solution for your publishing needs too—the "Instant Publishing Machine." Behind the scenes, Brendon Burchard has been using this process for almost two years for his books, *The Millionaire Messenger* and *The Charge*, as well as for his audio books. We modeled Brendon's ingenious strategies right into the system with his permission. I think Brendon is the SMARTEST author marketer in the world right now. He truly wants to see people succeed, so he's given us some of his best strategies to share with you!

We've designed the process to be extremely simple for you. Fill in the blanks, press a button, and you've got an instant book-selling website. However, what makes the system really magical is that after a buyer orders your book from Amazon, Barnes and Noble or another publisher and forwards their receipt to the site, the customer will automatically get a bonus video, audio, or training program. This gives you... a list of buyer leads. And remember, *your list is your currency.*

Anyone who's invested in your book is an ideal candidate to buy your products... and then more of your products.

So, what if you don't have a product?

Maybe you don't right now, but you will.

We have a system for that too! It's called the "Instant Product Machine," and it's designed to step-by-step turn your knowledge into a viable product you can sell.

Fill in the blanks, upload your product, and sell it for whatever price you want. The Instant Product Machine captures payments and automatically delivers your product to the customer's mobile phone, tablet, desktop, or laptop computer.

We provide a direct interface with Amazon and Paypal so you get paid instantly.

No technical skills required. If you can fill out an online form, you can do this.

Make money while you sleep.

But, it doesn't stop there. You've got to get the word out there and create buzz to generate even more leads. And, guess what?

We have a solution for this also—the "Instant Promotion Machine."

This is the same system Darren Hardy, publisher of Success Magazine, used to build a list exceeding 200,000 people in less than a year. It captures names, email addresses, and phone numbers. It even asks your prospects questions and lets you communicate with email, mobile text, audio, and video messages. This is your *list*. This is your *platform*. This is your *currency*.

There's one more step. Profit. And our "Instant Profit Machine" makes this step super easy too. When you use our system, we're going to promote your book and product in our online store, which gives you access to hundreds of thousands of international prospects and customers.

Imagine what it would be like to be on vacation, sitting on a beach or sailing the Pacific, while you're making money. It's possible. And you can do it.

These marketing machines create a cycle that results in an even bigger list, more sales, better products, rich stories of transformation that generate substance and proof, increased media coverage, and exponential profits.

 # It's (Finally) Your Time to Shine

So, let's do this.

Imagine what your life would be like if you were able to obtain financial freedom by sharing what you love with the world. Think about what this can do for your career, your life, and the people you want to profoundly help.

Whatever the vision is that makes you feel completely fulfilled and whatever the dollar amount you need to make that happen—it's within your reach.

Get the jumpstart you've always wanted. Begin generating meaningful content, think of new, innovative ways to solve people's problems, and start pursuing your passion.

It's your time to shine.

It's your time to be a star.

Let's Dance :)

There's an old saying we all know.

It's time to *do something* or get off the pot.

You're looking into a crystal ball right now—it's what I believe is the "Next Big Thing." We've entered into a "perfect storm" of technology, knowledge, a shift in power, distribution, media, politics, banking and world attitudes.

There's only one way to ensure your financial safety, security, independence and growth.

Your platform.

Every PERSON on the PLANET Needs a Platform.

Every single business,
Every single person on the planet,
Needs a platform and a system to increase their value.

If you're SATISFIED making ⅕ of what you could be, then hesitate and wait...and pay the price by getting further pushed down into being seen as a commodity.

Do you want to be the person who missed out on the big Real Estate boom in the early 2000s (before the prices went sky-high)? Or missed out buying Apple Stock when it was $20 a share?

It doesn't need to happen to you again. You can get on the big opportunity and ride the wave of what I believe is the missing piece, the system and process you need to get you from where you are to where you want to go.

Watch the video at
www.AuthorExpertMarketingMachines.com

It's your time to shine.
It's your time to be a star.
This is Mike Koenigs, and I'll see you on the other side.

About MIKE KOENIGS

#1 Bestselling Author, "2009 Marketer of the Year", entrepreneur, filmmaker, speaker and patented inventor of "Cross-Channel" Marketing Technology.

Mike is the CEO (Chief Disruptasaurus) and Founder of Traffic Geyser and Instant Customer. His products simplify marketing for tens of thousands of small businesses, authors, experts, speakers, coaches and consultants worldwide.

His celebrity and bestselling author clients and friends include Paula Abdul, Tony Robbins, Tim Ferriss, Debbie Ford, Brian Tracy, Jorge Cruise, Dan Kennedy, Harvey MacKay, and John Assaraf from "The Secret".

Traffic Geyser distributes video, articles and media to nearly 100 different social media and social networking platforms with the press of a button that automates marketing while saving small business owners days or weeks of time and thousands of dollars in promoting their business.

Instant Customer is an automated "cross-channel" marketing platform that captures leads with voice recognition, mobile, online and offline systems – dramatically simplifying and reducing the cost of marketing for small business owners in over 60 different countries.

For over 20 years, Mike has created and implemented innovative, high-tech, and high-touch marketing campaigns for companies like Sony Entertainment, 20th Century Fox, 3M, General Mills, Dominos Pizza, BMW, Ralston and Mazda.

Mike's companies have produced eight consecutive seven-figure online product launches; the largest launch grossed over $9.1 million and made over $3.1 million in sales during a "direct to camera" live webcast.

Mike is the author of the #1 Bestselling book "Author Expert Marketing Machines" and "Instant Customer Revolution", a book about how to become a highly paid small business-marketing consultant with cutting-edge mobile, video and social media tools.

He executive produced "Bill's Gun Shop", an independent feature film that was distributed by Warner Brothers. He also produced a feature documentary, "LifeWithTesla" about living gas-free with an electric car charged by the Sun. That documentary is available free at www.LifeWithTesla.com.

Originally from Eagle Lake, Minnesota, Mike lives in San Diego, California with his wife and son. He loves the ocean, is an avid boater, fisherman, and plays the "didgeridoo" and a variety of other instruments. He strongly dislikes the smell and taste of canned tuna, egg salad and Brussels sprouts.

Mike can be reached through his personal web site at www.MikeKoenigs.com.

Connect With Me

Facebook: www.FaceBook.com/koenigs
Twitter: @MikeKoenigs
Linked In: www.linkedin.com/in/mikekoenigs
YouTube: www.YouTube.com/KoenigsMike
Google Plus: plus.Google.com/+MikeKoenigs

The Fine Print*

the one our attorney wants us to share with you :(

The content, case studies and examples shared in this ebook do not in any way represent the "average" or "typical" member experience. In fact, as with any product or service, we know that some members purchase our systems and never use them, and therefore get no results from their membership whatsoever. You should assume that you will obtain no results with this program. Therefore, the member case studies we are sharing can neither represent nor guarantee the current or future experience of other past, current or future members. Rather, these member case studies represent what is possible with our system. Each of these unique case studies, and any and all results reported in these case studies by individual members, are the culmination of numerous variable, many of which we cannot control, including pricing, target market conditions, product/service quality, offer, customer service, personal initiative, and countless other tangible and intangible factors.

Whether this Notice refers to "you," "your," or "user," it means "you," while "we" or "our" refers to VoiceFollowUp, LLC dba Instant Customer ("IC").

Any earnings or income statements, or earnings income examples, are only estimates of what we think you could earn. There is no assurance you'll do as well. If you rely upon our figures, you must accept the risk of not doing as well.

Where specific income figures are used, and attributed to an individual or business, those persons or businesses have earned that amount. There is no assurance you'll do as well. If you rely upon our figures, you must accept the risk of not doing as well.

Moreover, where specific website traffic or search engine ranking results are used and attributed to an individual or business, those persons or businesses have achieved those results. There is no assurance you'll do as well. If you rely upon our figures, you must accept the risk of not doing as well.

Any and all claims or representations, regarding income earnings on www.AuthorExpertMarketingMachines.com, are not considered to be as average earnings. Likewise, any and all claims or representations, as to web site traffic or search engine ranking results on www.AuthorExpertMarketingMachines.com, are not to be considered as average results.

There can be no assurance that any prior successes, or past results, regarding income earnings, website traffic or search engine ranking results can be used as an indication of your future success or results.

Monetary and income results are based on many factors. We have no way of knowing how well will do, as we do not know you, your background, your work ethic, or your business skills or practices. Therefore we do not guarantee or imply that you will get rick, that you will do as well, or make any money at all. There is no assurance you'll do as well. If you rely upon our figures, you must accept the risk of not doing as well.

Likewise, website traffic or search engine ranking results are based on many factors. We have no way of knowing how well you will do, as we do not know you, your background, your work ethic, or your business skills or practices. Therefore we do not guarantee or imply that you will get traffic, that you will do as well, or achieve website traffic or optimal search engine rankings at all. There is no assurance you'll do as well. If you reply upon your figures, you must accept the risk of not doing as well.

Internet businesses and earnings derived there from, have unknown risks involved, and are not suitable for everyone. Making decisions based on any information presented in our products, service, or website, should be done only with the knowledge that you could experience significant losses, make no money at all, or achieve no desired results regarding website traffic or search engine rankings at all.

Products on www.AuthorExpertMarketingMachines.com are for educational and informational purposes only. Use caution and seek the advice of qualified professionals. Check with your accountant, lawyer, or professional advisor, before acting on this or any information.

Users of our products, services and website are advised to do their own due diligence when it comes to making business decisions and all information, products, and services that have been provided should be independently verified by your own qualified professional. Our information, products and services on www.AuthorExpertMarketingMachines.com should be carefully considered and evaluated, before reaching a business decision, on whether to rely on them.

You agree that our companies are not responsible for the success or failure of your business decisions relating to any information presented by www.AuthorExpertMarketingMachines.com, or our companies' products or services.

IT'S YOUR TIME TO SHINE.

Are you an author, expert, speaker, consultant, coach or entrepreneur? Have you ever wanted to get published as an author? Be perceived as the "go to" expert or authority in your niche? Attract media attention? Have products that can be sold to make money while you sleep? Finally get paid as much as you're worth? In fact, have you ever wanted to be a star?

Let's face it…we all have. Until now, however, there just hasn't been a blueprint for how to do it easily, quickly and effectively.

Author Expert Marketing Machines represents decades of experience from the best-of-the-best in their respective fields—incredibly successful authors, speakers, coaches and consultants—who have broken through, and have successfully published and built profitable businesses and brands, all around their unique expertise and personality.

In this groundbreaking five step system, Mike Koenigs brings you the step-by-step blueprint for how to do it, the automated tools to get you there fast, and the wisdom and examples from dozens of people who have done it successfully in an incredibly diverse array of fields.

Not only is it possible to make your dreams happen, it's your birthright. Now, with Author Expert Marketing Machines you have the system that will show you how.

About Mike Koenigs

Author, Founder & Creator of Author Expert Marketing Machines
Mike Koenigs is a #1 Bestselling author, "2009 Marketer of the Year" winner, entrepreneur, filmmaker, speaker, author and holds a patent in "Cross-Channel" Marketing Technology. He is the CEO and "Chief-Disruptasaurus" of Traffic Geyser and Instant Customer. His products simplify marketing for tens of thousands of small businesses, authors, experts, speakers, coaches and consultants worldwide. Mike is on a crusade to create 1,000,000 entrepreneurs and 1,000,000 millionaires with his tools training and systems.